EAGLE'S PASS

A Collection of Poems by
Darinka Springer

A.H. STOCKWELL
PUBLISHERS SINCE 1898

Published in 2023 by
Darinka Springer
in association with
Arthur H Stockwell Ltd
West Wing Studios
Unit 166, The Mall
Luton, Bedfordshire
ahstockwell.co.uk

British Library Cataloguing-in-Publication Data
A catalogue record for this book is
available from the British Library.
ISBN: 9780722352977

The views and opinions expressed herein belong to the author and do not necessarily reflect those of AH Stockwell

Dedicated to my guardian angel

Contents

Dedicated to my guardian angel

Contents

He has given His angels charge over thee;
to keep thee in all thy ways.
In their hands
He shall bear thee up;
lest thou dash
thy foot against a stone

—Psalm 91: 11-12

Prologue

It is past Midnight,
New Year 2022

Oh, angel,
my guardian
refresh my soul
with divine poetry

You are the thread
that keeps together
my life's tapestry

Eagle's Pass

Cave Poems: XII

Peaks of my mountains
changed into
orange light

Peaks of my mountains
are bright
by The Host

Will there always be
orange light

Is it possible
to live
without these mountains
for one's happiness

Cave Poems: XVI

Bunch of heather
on the altar
on your wounded heart
for doubting Thomas
for Mary Magdalene
Nicodem and Peter in order
that we shall believe
become whole
to know the truth

On your wounded heart
24hr application
the same thanks
with accomplishment
of adoration

your wound
is opening into the wonderful land
to bring it
here to us

Cave Poems: Interment

When you look
beyond the plains
of wheat

And put your ears
to the virginal wind
I shall be with you
in the song
of summer

Look after the earth
of growing wheat
Give hand
to the wind
who will pass
my window

Cave Poems: The Cross

In repose of consolation
I await you
as does grain
in the early morning rain
turns in transmutation

For the glints of light
glisten, glitter white
from the sight
of crucifixion

Confirmation of Faith

I am not
about my dreams

I am not
about what was wrong

I am not
about what I thought was right

I am only
a possibility
through which
the light
of God's love
is able
to shine through

This is
who I am

Inspired by Boby Shuller and John Newton

The Questions

How is it that
what it is
disappears

How is it that
what is not yet
becomes

How is it that
laughter
ends in tears

The inner child
is growing up
and hears
her own cry
why?

Through the gap
of her heart
she saw
the blue sky
and embraced it

That's why.

Reflecting Diamond

A man
became the man
when he had started
to make toys
and worship idols

As a collecting
genius
he expressed
within himself
his inherent
religion

The evolution
of the concept
of God
began
branching off
into philosophy
& theology.

God save religion!

P.S. Not only
working tools
instigated man's evolution

A Simple Prayer

Thank you God
for the exercise,
for the walk,
for the talk
& breath of fresh air

You are my rock
I am allowed
to knock
on your door
and rewind
my clock
for evermore

Childlike

She bought
her teddy bear
in Knightsbridge
in the year 2010
and called him
Harrods-Knight-Bear

Her life was not
24 carat gold
but her sense of humour
kept her bold

There is a rumour
that it is cool
to be childlike
and free
when old
to inherit
the kingdom of light
and its gold;

Sleep tight
sleep well
my Harrods-Knight.

A Little Chat

Grand Daughter asked her
Grand Mother
"What is the most impressive
sentence in The Old Testament
Granny?"

Granny replied "It is not good for the man
to be alone"
"And what advice could you
take from the scriptures in a
nutshell?" said the girl

"If you maul the world
you will crawl
for a long future" was the
reply

"How touching it makes me cry"
Grand Daughter responded
"It is written in your heart
that's why you feel this way
bless you" said Granny

Senior Moments

Leaves were yellow
and maroon
strewn
across her view
the true
beauty of autumn

With grandeur
she had to surrender
to the wonder
sublime and be thine

It is not
early any more
to close
the retail store
to veer into the great
unknown

Faith does facilitate
the journey

now please
open the gate

Thank you!

Mirror Image

She wrote
the end
before she has scribbled
the beginning

In eternity
everything is
the other way around

Crescendo

Ink fades
paper decays
gossip moves away
details are lost
memories shrink
the truth is denied
at the end
all is sleeping
seemingly dies
becomes alive
elsewhere
into a new life

Feeling good
hinged
on precarious
balance of an internal
dialogue
and an external
event

Nothing to Declare Except

Anxiety
Apathy
Aspiration
Failings
Forgetfulness
Lethargy
Longing
Memories
Shortcomings
Stupidity
Body – Mind
Faith – Hope – love

Customs free
because of Jesus

P.S. Reflecting on Cardinal Henry Newman saying:
His cross brought together and "made consistent
all that seems discordant and aimless"

Evanescent Moments

Over the time
all is gone
like dreams
with igniting
waves

Green cry
purple echo
and I
soaking crust
of toast

Yearning
for a thunder
vanished

Under the sky
the speed
licked
my tongue

Many aeons
will bloom
spacious
nothingness
serene
and speechless…

Awakening

When fires frizzle
and yawns
roam free
rekindling
starts again
with thee

You are
by golden candle
that makes me
glow inside
with pride

Grant me
your wisdom
to be
a pen
in my step
and lead me
out of my nap
to a happy
afterlife

Faith

Teach me
to see the world
in true proportion
discerning
the beauty
beneath
apparent
ruthlessness

Confer on me
uncoverable
hope

Assure me
even in the hour
of desolation
that you are there
to care
for me

Make me
believe
in such attainment

Fate

With a bit of luck
I shan't be stuck
with dimunition
of myself

If

Gods providence
is there
nature
will know
where
to go
on the shelf
of probability

Perpetually

To be
without you
it is
not to be
at all

Ever after
has no cause
to be
begotten

Totality
of which I am
composed
eternity
to which
I belong
have no life
without you

Like a song
touched
by the voice
of a poet
something special
unites me
with you

A Penny for a Thought

Many a sod
think they are God

A folly
is like a broken
brolly
on a rainy day

Alike the tower
of a mock
gothic ruins;
the folly

Two Pennies to Rub Together

It is nothing wrong
to have a splash
of dosh
o gosh
cash
is not
a trash

When
a penny drops
more ways
than one

it would be prudent
to have
some fun

Ha ha on a day
keeps the doctor away

The Verdict:
life is sometimes
Harvey Nichols
sometimes
pickles

A Jolly Good Party

Cats meowed
Dogs woofed
Goats bleated
Pigs snorted
Ducks quacked
Pigeons cooed
Cows mooed
Birds trilled
Donkeys made
hee haw sounds
Yet there was
no audience around
until
Bells tolled
Drinking glasses
reverberated

Behold!
Fingers pressed
on intercom
Hands knocked
on the door
Guitar strings
strummed
Bees outside
hummed in glory
and everything was
hunky dory

The Secret

I hope
I shall not be
too late
with my credentials
at the gate.
Z-88

Humbling
humbling and painful
the truth
of separation sounds
and I am not in a hurry

As the fashion
of this world
passes away
my inner world
with the spirit
of the Lord
is no longer grey

Thank you
for keeping my heart
to beat;
if in future
I'll have to change
my seat
I hope
you'll make
my ends to meet

Eagle's Pass

"The eagle has landed"
said the onlookers from the other side

"It seems that way"
reviled one among them
"but it is actually a crow"

"Don't be daft"
commented the second soul
"it is only a sparrow, but it is important that it has made it"

All the souls were consoled
"Thanks be to god" they exclaimed

"His eye is on the sparrow"

Reminder

As the telomere
a protective cap
is to the chromosome

So it is
my prayer
a godomere
a protective shield
to my faith

An Observation

Walking
on the life's
narrow lane
we cudgel
our brain
how to live
the best
at the behest
of the universal law
and clutch
the straw
when drowning

Guidelines

Beware without a stare
don't drink wine where there is a fine

Overlook others mistakes
thus unlook yours

Don't play the Pope
if you can't spell church

Don't tinker and muck around
if you are a lousy thinker

Don't be a plumber
if you are a dumber

Don't try to be a cook
if butter would not melt in your mouth.

If you are short of dough
don't open a bakery

If you cannot get your head around it
find a new chapter or a new chaplain

If you are painstakingly clever and bright
you will be to many
cat's whiskers delight

Let not your heart burn
if you'll be stowed in the urn.

If bread and butter can't be bettered
we have to be grateful with one's lot (with what we have)

Commandments

Don't cast your dosh
Just to be posh

Don't put on weight
if you want to look great

Don't cast your brain
just to be vain

Don't cast your toothbrush
in a rush

Don't cast your old friend
for a new trend

Do love yourself even as an elf

Don't waste your speech
on a leech

Don't waste your money
on a false "honey"

Love your pun
on the short or long run

Be on your guard
with a lions heart
yet not hard of hearing
when there is
a cry for help somewhere

Proverbially

To have everything
for the few
is better
than nothing
for everyone

To be happy
and not knowing
is better
than knowing
unhappiness

Genuine cry
is better
than false
laughter

Not to do good
is better
than to do bad

Breadcrumbs

A

I walked
through Kensington Gardens
saw a tree
whose branches
were kneeling
down to the ground
I was bound to the feeling
of a cosmic spirit
without a sound

B

Fortnum & Mason
makes a common man
an aristocrat,
its food
gilds our palette
so when we are
in the Green Park
our mood
takes us there
said Clark and Claire
O'Boy said also
my friend Roy

C

I observed
a tiny slug
on my window sill
and suddenly
felt sluggish
it is not
a skin off my nose
(or under)
I said to myself
and let it be
free

D

The church bells
at St Pauls Cathedral
peal
thus steal
my heart
in jubilation (2022)
I shall seal
those moments of joy
in platinum

Trivia

A

Some days I felt like

A cheque book
without funds

A coffee
without a cup

A map
without a car

Spectacles
without eyes

An aroma
without a nose

A table cloth
without a table

A curtain
without a window

A wine glass
without a wine

A glass of wine
without a mouth

Like urine
without a bladder

A ladder
without a climber

A freezer
in a cold country

Yet like a heater
in hot weather

To be an ink
without a pen
is like a thought
without a thinker

B

Would it be cheeky
to give a peck
on one's cheeks.

"As long as you have
a chic mirror"

said the mirror

Gnarls

A

To see
the funny side
of life
is to add
youthfulness
to an old age

Like a sage
longing for youth
it is not
uncouth

It is a memory bank
in the roots
of an aged tree
on the long
river bank
a shank
of mortality

B

Look at your life
with relaxing
smile
for do's and don'ts

With the shoes on
or bare
go an extra mile

Enjoy your break
with a venison steak
and say;
thanks god
"for let one be in the U.K."

A Garment of Decay

By the time
my life is over
the moth will eat
all of my pullover

Nothing will
go to waste
when I become
earths paste

It is great
to have a gift
of life
albeit in constant
strife

I wish to believe
that God is there
to renew my ticket
for life's fare

When I go down
the escalator of life
to the pit of extinction
enable me, o God
the flight of stairs
toward the naked light
of yours

" I am who I am"

On Self Reflection

The body
said to another body

"I am nobody"

The other body replied
"I also have the mind
because I mind my own business
I mind the stairs and where I am going"

The first body then said
"Thanks for reminding me, how I am somebody"

Pilgrimage

Barefoot
on the Pilgrim's journey
of life
with arrows
of faith
hope
and love
in my quiver

Approaching the shrine
with reluctance

Dear Angel
will you stand
by me
at the moment
of epiphany?

An Apology

I have been around in this world for over seventy years

So many microscopically perfect creatures were living at
the same time and I never gave it enough thought

I am so sorry
I've missed so much

now in a decade or so
I have to depart

I am guilty of omission
may I be absolved

I was in the world
whether bored, lonely, lively, happy or sad
I should've looked closer

This was my sin indeed
God of universe
please accept my contribution
with love and remorse

Yours Truly, Darinka

Declaration

I have not
enough faith
to be
an atheist

have I had
such faith
it would be
a nail
in my coffin

No two ways
about it

Epitaph

A

And you will remain
the autumn
rustling
in my poems

and you will reign
for ever
my freedom

and you will
claim me
on the day
of judgement

B

We lost
the sense
of holiness
in all things

The gratitude
for life
while living

This was our
most original
sin

May we be
forgiven

The Wheel of Samsara

Everything has changed
except God and me

Did I wish
no longer to exist
that final doubt
to which
God himself
might humble
one day?

For that something
I was afraid
it existed
and the terrible;
did I wish
no longer to exist
of that final doubt

Nothing has changed
except god and me

*Published by Regency Press 1976 – editors choice –
anthology of selected contemporary verse.*

Reconnecting

15.8.2022

Molecular echo
on the surface marks
of reality

Looking at your photo
my dear mama
I am kissing
your blessed
shadow

I feel your presence
on the waves
of self-awareness

In the depth
of your eyes
is a remnant
of my soul
you have taken it
with you
when you departed
to heaven

Sunrise Call

Give the chance a chance
Let the probability to have a choice
Do not let an incident be an accident
Make happiness happen
Strive for favourable coincidence
Things that come suddenly are gradual in making
Let your slow be fast and fast slow
To know the truth it's not a piece of cake, but it can be a peace of mind
To be amidst the civilisation, it's a privilege, a cause for celebration
When one is lost, even a faded sign is welcome
Tears of joy are the crowning glory of a self-conscious being
As soon as words are written, they will dwindle, such is life
Go for it and let it go, distinguish the difference
Emoji with a smile ☺ and Emoji with a sour face ☹
Got married at their wedding, they ate sweet and
sour chicken, yummy, how appropriate.

The Stickers

They were asked one by one
"What have you got to say about yourself"
and they all replied accordingly to their status

The Shoemaker – I am on a shoestring
The Shoe – It is down at heel
The Tailor – It is tailor made
The Suit – It suits you
The Beautician – It is a lip service
The Nail – Nail down
The Head – Head over heels
The Brain – Brain box
The Logician – It's logical
The Thinker – It makes one think
The Speaker – I am lost for words
The Word – Take my word for it
The Truth – It's gospel truth
The Book – It's a long story
The Mouth – By the word of the mouth
The Astronomer – I am over the moon
The Scientist – It's a hard nut to crack
The Believer – It's unbelievable
The Psychologist – It's not all it seems
The G.P. – It is a headache
The Musician – I can't face the music
The Humorist – Don't make me laugh
The Cook – I am full of beans
The Waiter – Wait a bit
The Servant – It serves your turn
The Footballer – It's a goal

The Plumber – It's nuts and bolts
The Dancer – One step at a time
The Butcher to the Vegetarian – It is a bone
of contention, I work to the bone
The Driver – It's miles away
The Window Cleaner – Wipe the slate clean
The Runner – I am running out of hope
The Barber – It's a short cut
The Stuffed Shirt – Get stuffed
The Silence – Silence is golden
The Pleasure – At your pleasure
The Earth – It costs the earth
The Case – Just in case
The Grass – It's greener on the other side
The Time – Time will tell, give it time
The Wine Glass – Cheers
The Mouse – It's a trap
The Rabbit – Rabbit and pork.
The Wolf – Keep the wolf from the door
The Sheep – I feel sheepish
The Cat – It's cat's pyjamas
The Pen – I'll make a note of it
The Toy – I am toying with the idea
The Hill – Over the hill
The Devil – Go to hell
God – God knows